Traeger Grill & Smoker Recipes

The Cookbook with Tasty BBQ
Recipes to Enjoy Smoking with
Your Traeger Grill

DAVID EVANS

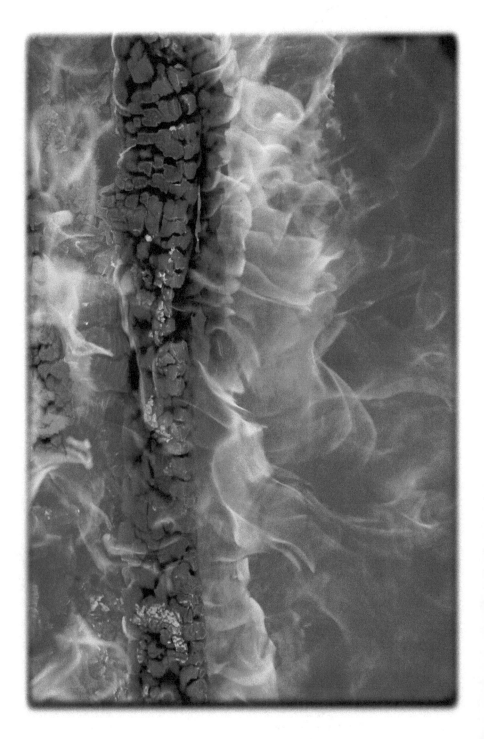

Contents

Introduction

If you like to eat barbecue on a summer night and linger on the mouthwatering tang of the best-smoked burgers, spare ribs, or timber fried noodles afterward, Traeger Grill s is the correct location for you. There's the north run of the mill roughly Traeger Grill s. It's always been recognized among the very best on earth with its sumptuous al fresco Traeger Grill systems. They don't use charcoal or gas to supply better and healthy choices by applying indirect heat in preparing meals. As opposed to utilizing propane or charcoal, Traeger Grill s utilizes a quarter-inch wood pellet that looks a good deal like giant horse pills and may quickly and burn approximately 8500 BTUs per pound produce their beef, vegetables, and fish hot and packed with flavor. A particular high temperature is required to cook the hamburgers and hotdogs perfectly. On the flip side, cooking varied meals like fish, poultry, brisket, and poultry entails a suitable method in supervising the warmth to prevent undercook food.

What's more, Traeger Grill s showcase direct and safe means of the cook. Throughout indirect cook, the food is split out of the fire us a barrier. Accord to experts, cook meals not directly produce flexibility as it offers a person the capability to correct or place in timber to accommodate an individual's flavor of meals. By comparison, cook meals directly utilize no obstacles so that it may lead to overcooked food. Direct Traeger Grill can cause burn and charr of meals, which makes it unhealthy to consume and may result in undesirable health issues. The conversion from amino acids into carcinogens cancer-because chemicals may happen. This is precisely what makes Traeger Grill s distinctive and different. The Traeger pellet Traeger Grill s is an ideal option if you would like to invest quality time with your nearest and dearest and revel in flavorsome food. These Traeger Grill s is made to offer a healthful and secure alternative in cook since it utilizes natural wood pellets rather than charcoal or gas.

Additionally, it uses indirect heat when cooked to prevent charred food, leading to cancer or injury to our body and reducing the number of fats from the meals while creating the superb smoky tang. With it, you do not need to be bothered about the health hazard and mess. Moreover, its automated system makes these users friendly and convenient. You do not need to devote a good deal of time view over the Traeger Grill; instead, you have to begin the Traeger Grill and place the necessary temperature to cook your meals.

Purchasing Guide for a Traeger Grill
While purchase a Traeger Grill, a considerable portion of your choice will depend upon your budget and what you are able. Just remember that based on how many times you utilize your Traeger, you will also have to devote a couple of hundred dollars per year, or even more, for wood pellets to run your Traeger Grill. How many folks do you expect to cook? The number of people may decide how large of a barbecue you purchase. For a household of two adults and two children, or much less, I believe that you can handle any of the more significant sized Traeger Grill s. For larger families or households with older kids that consume more, the larger Traeger Grill

dimensions are likely a much better match since you're able to manage more meals simultaneously. Also, think about where you anticipate placing your Traeger Grill. You may be fortunate enough to have a condominium that permits Traeger Grill son balconies. However, your patio may only have sufficient room to accommodate a giant-sized Traeger Grill. Traeger has made this choice an easy one for you to browse since they have included the Traeger Grill capability right in the title of every Traeger Grill. The number after the Traeger Grill version consistently indicates the size of this Traeger Grill capability in square inches.

To put it differently, the Ironwood 880 includes 880 square inches of the Traeger Grill area. The Guru 780 contains 780 square inches of the Traeger Grill area. The Timberline 1300 includes 1300 square inches of the Traeger Grill area. Remember, the larger the Traeger Grill, the longer pellets it will have to heat it. Consequently, if you believe you're merely likely to be cook for two or three people regularly, you may be west cash on pellets seek to warm up a giant Traeger Grill.

On the contrary, it may be a better choice to obtain the Traeger Grill and apply the sav s towards more pellets. In my view, this is among the most significant factors as it is mostly going to ascertain what size and features you want. If you seek to throw a block party or cookout with different racks of ribs, pork butts, or large briskets, then a larger Traeger Grill more inner property is best to accommodate the more oversized format of those cuts of beef. Each of the series includes two Traeger Grill dimensions: a bigger one and a bigger one. The Traeger Grill s in each line are always cheaper than the larger ones, as anticipated. More about the detailed comparisons under. It is essential to understand that every Traeger essentially works the same. They use the power to burn 100% organic timber pellets that are engineered. There's not any gas, natural gas, or charcoal included. All you will need is access to an electric socket and Traeger-brand wood pellets. Unlike many traditional Traeger Grill s, Traeger utilizes indirect heat for cook meals (no direct heat or flame-to-food cook). The fire pit has a heated pole and little fan. Since the pellets get warm from the bar, the enthusiast introduces oxygen along with the pellets glow. Above it's the greased pan, which grabs any drip s that drop while the food cooks, and transmits it to some skillet or bucket.

The simplest way to understand that a Traeger would be to consider it as an outside convection oven with Traeger Grill, smoke, Traeger Grill, and back abilities. It's by far the most versatile and user-friendly barbecue I've ever cooked with. The Pro Series Traeger Grill s will be the most economical. The Timberline is the costliest, and also, the Ironwood is someplace in between. You are purchasing a Traeger Grill is sort of like buying a vehicle. You may buy the baseline version, which includes regular features, the midline version with a sunroof and leather chairs, or even the fully-loaded variant that accompanies each of the above and a 21-speaker sound system, 20" chrome rims, along with a larger engine. Each update includes a cost. If you only have the budget for the entry Professional Str or top-of-the-line Timberline, I honestly think You're making a Superb decision purchase a Traeger.

Tips for Maintaining Your Traeger Grill

When triggered, creosote makes a scorching flame. Airborne dust particles will undergo the cook room, and a few of these airborne contaminants will collect on the flue liner, very similar to creosote, which might be conducive to some flame. The smokestack exhaust should be inspected at least two times per year to ascertain when a creosote or grease buildup has happened. Additionally, grease drip s in the meals will fall on the dirt drain pan and be emptied to the dirt drain and then from the Traeger Grill throughout the dust drain tube to accumulate in the skillet. Grease will collect in everyone these locations. The dirt drain, the dirt drain tube, and the dust bucket ought to be inspected at least two times per year for grease buildup signs. Once creosote or grease has been collected, it should be eliminated to decrease fire probability. Remove (unscrew) the chimney cap assembly on the surface of the flue pipe. When the chimney cap assembly was eliminated, it may be washed us warm, soapy water with a biodegradable degreaser. Scrape the creosote and dirt accumulation from the interior of the horizontal and vertical segments of the flue pipe with a rigid, nonmetallic instrument. A wooden paint stir rod, by way of instance, would function for this particular undertaking. When the creosote and dirt residue have been loosened in the flue pipe liner, a lot of it could be eliminated with paper towels or disposable rags. Don't spray water or liquid cleansers on the interior of your

Traeger Grill. When the flue pipe was cleaned, then replace the chimney cap assembly.

Accumulated grease is simpler to wash off when the Traeger Grill is still warm--not hot. Take care not to burn off. Gently wash out the dirt from this V-shaped dirt drain and grease drain tube. If an excessive amount of grease is permitted to accumulate from the V-shaped grease drain or plug in the dirt drain tub, a grease fire can result. We recommend clean these places regularly. Eliminate the porcelain-coated Traeger Grill grates along with the dirt drain pan. This will give access to this V-shaped grease drain and grease drain tube opens within the Traeger Grill. Scrape the dirt accumulation from within the conical dirt drain and grease drain tube with a rigid, nonmetallic instrument. Many of this loosened dirt can be pushed through the dirt drain tube and slip into the dirt bucket. Wipe up remaining dirt residue with paper towels or disposable rags. Paper towels or disposable rags may also be used to wash some of the dirt from the Grill's inside surfaces inside surfaces. Line your earth bucket us aluminum foil for simple cleanup. Empty is sometimes based on the quantity of usage. Change the aluminum foil onto the dirt drain pan regularly (sometimes after every use, determined by which has been cooked).

Clean Your Traeger Grill
A Traeger Grill was designed to continue provided that you keep and run it securely continuously. What's more, you always have to wash it regularly to get rid of the build-up of carbon and dirt accumulation. Nobody would like to taste rancid dirt or rancid carbon in their

majestically cooked legumes or fish kebabs. Whenever dirt burns, it generates acrid smoke, which can mess up your food. Before you cook, you have to do some cleanup to maintain your Traeger Grill or Traeger Grill is act   in a great state, prevent off-flavors, and prolong your stove's life span. Then, the system requires maintenance and comprehensive cleanup. Should you always use that, then you want to do a thorough clean three or four times annually before story it to get winter? These hints below will direct you on how to wash a Traeger Grill efficiently. Spray the dirt catch bucket utilize vegetable spray once you're prepared to drain it. Afterward, the drip s will slip out easily. Take a few paper towels so that you can swab the inside of your bucket.

Drain the dirt once the weather is warm on a more regular basis. Therefore, it doesn't turn rancid. Or place into a cottage cheese container and then toss it out as necessary. The simplest way of clean your ceramic coated grids would be for one to have a bit of aluminum foil and rub it over the grids. Be careful not to burn yourself! Take advantage of a long sleeve forehead mitt so you can guard your hand and forearm. Vacuum outside your pellet ash from around and in the firepot and underside of your cook room. It is possible to use a vegetable brush to remove built a scale onto the interior of your Traeger Grill. The simplest way of massive cleans the cook grids will be to set them within the self-clean oven and then turn the knob to begin the cleanup. Both the range and cook grids will be sterile without have a great deal of elbow grease. This is very helpful when the cook grids are encrusted with the residue of meals.

Another way of clean the cook grids is by merely putting them in an extreme yard debris bag. You include one-half cup of ammonia and then seal the bag shut. Lay the cook grids level immediately. Eliminate the grids the following day, thoroughly rinse with warm water, and they'll be fine and very tidy. The ammonia helps to dissolve the dirt on the cook grids. If you're experiencing a stainless steel Traeger Grill, then never forget to dust off the Traeger Grill before you begin to cook. It is possible to use a moist cloth to conduct this job. Otherwise, the dirt will cook in the metal and only discolor it. Be sure the foil is closely wrapped around the borders to help maintain even airflow.

Halibut Marinated with Red Wine
Ingredients

- 1 Large Clove Garlic
- 2 Teaspoons Red Wine Vinegar
- ½ Cup Extra-Virgin Olive Oil
- ¼ Teaspoon Red Pepper Flakes
- 4 Halibut Fillets, 1 To 1¼ Inches Thick (About 6 Ounces Each), Skin Removed
- Salsa Verde
- ¼ Cup Extra-Virgin Olive Oil
- 2 Teaspoons Freshly Grated Lemon Zest
- ½ Teaspoon Kosher or Sea Salt
- 1 Cup Loosely Packed Fresh Flat-Leaf Parsley Leaves
- 2 Tablespoons Capers, Rinsed and Drained
- 2 Oil-Packed Anchovy Fillets, Patted Dry and Minced

Instructions

- Prepare a medium-hot fire in a charcoal Traeger Grill or preheat a gas Traeger Grill on medium high. In a back   dish large enough to hold the halibut in a s le layer, combine the ¼ cup olive oil, the lemon zest, salt, and red pepper flakes.
- Stir to blend thoroughly. Add the halibut fillets and turn to coat both sides. Set aside. While the Traeger Grill is heat, make the salsa: In a food processor fitted with the metal blade, combine the

parsley, capers, anchovies, garlic, and vinegar and process until minced.

- With the machine run, add the ½ cup olive oil through the feed tube and process until emulsified. Transfer the salsa to a bowl and set aside. Oil the Traeger Grill grate. Use tongs to arrange the halibut fillets, flesh side down, directly over the medium-hot fire and cover.
- Traeger Grill the halibut until Traeger Grill marks are etched across the fillets, about 3 minutes.
- Turn the fillets and re-cover the Traeger Grill. Cook until the halibut is almost opaque throughout but still very moist when tested with a knife, or an instant-read thermometer inserted in the center registers 125° to 130°F, 2 to 3 minutes longer. Us tongs or a wide spatula, transfer the fillets to warmed dinner plates, and accompany each fillet with a spoonful of the salsa. Serve immediately.

Black Pepper Salmon with Orange Juice
Ingredients

- 1 Large Lime
- 100ml Freshly Squeezed Lemon Juice
- 100ml Freshly Squeezed Orange Juice
- Olive Oil
- 4 Tablespoons Balsamic Vinegar
- 2 Teaspoons Freshly Chopped Dill
- 2 Large Garlic Cloves Divided
- Freshly Ground Black Pepper
- 4 Salmon Fillets with Skin Left On
- 2 Small Lemons
- 2 Medium Oranges
- Sea Salt
- 50ml Freshly Squeezed Lime Juice

Instructions

- Wash the salmon fillets thoroughly before then pat dry and drizzle   them with some olive oil and sprinkle   over them some sea salt and pepper on the skin side and rub it in. Then place in the refrigerator for 30 minutes. Cut the lemon, lime and oranges into segments make   sure that you retain as much of their juices as possible. Then mix these segments with some olive oil and ½ crushed garlic clove.
- Now place in the refrigerator. Next you need to combine the freshly cut dill with 1 garlic clove that has been crushed, the lime, lemon and orange juice and a little olive oil, salt and pepper. Once you have done this you remove the salmon fillets from

the refrigerator and place them in a shallow dish and pour over this marinade. Cover the dish and replace in the refrigerator and leave the salmon to marinate in the dill for at least 2 hours. Once two hours is up removing the salmon fillets from the refrigerator and as the barbecue warms up this will allow them to come up to room temperature. Allow the salmon to be out of the refrigerator for 20 minutes before you then place on the barbecue.

- Before you place the salmon on the barbecue rub the grate with a clove of garlic and then place the fish on it skin side down. After two minutes you must turn the salmon over and allow it to cook for a further two minutes.
- Also, it is important to place some sort of cover over the salmon such as saucepan lid that is well ventilated. Once cooked let the salmon fillets rest for 3 minutes before serve. When you serve the salmon place on the plate a small salad made up of lettuce, cherry tomatoes and drizzle some balsamic vinegar around the plate.

Crusted Halibut Chile-and-Peanut
Ingredients

- Cup Thai Lime and Chile Peanuts
- 4 Halibut Fillets, 1 To 1¼ Inches Thick (About 6 Ounces Each), Skin Removed
- 2 To 3 Tablespoons Extra-Virgin Olive Oil
- 1 Lime, Quartered

Instructions

- Prepare a medium-hot fire in a charcoal Traeger Grill or preheat a gas Traeger Grill on medium high. Arrange the halibut fillets on a rimmed back sheet and brush or rub on both sides with the olive oil. Put the peanuts in a heavy-duty lock-top plastic bag. Use a roll pin or the bottom of a small, heavy saucepan to crush the nuts finely. Crush them just enough to create small pieces without turn them to meal. Divide the nuts into 4 equal portions, and press a portion into the top, or flesh side, of each fillet, create a crust.
- To create a cool zone, bank the coals to one side of the Traeger Grill or turn off one of the burners. Oil the Traeger Grill grate. Us a spatula, transfer the halibut fillets, untrusted side up, directly over the medium-hot fire and cover.
- Traeger Grill the halibut until Traeger Grill marks are etched across the fillets, about 3 minutes. Use a spatula to move the fillets to the cool side of the Traeger Grill. Re-cover and Traeger Grill until the halibut is almost opaque throughout but still very moist when tested with a knife, or an instant-read

thermometer inserted in the center registers 125° to 130°F, 4 to 5 minutes longer. Us a spatula, transfer the fillets to warmed dinner plates, and place a lime wedge on each plate. Serve immediately.

Salted Halibut with Chipotle Sauce and Mayonnaise

Ingredients

- 2 Tablespoons Minced Fresh Cilantro
- ¼ Teaspoon Kosher or Sea Salt
- 4 Halibut Fillets, 1 To 1¼ Inches Thick (About 6 Ounces Each), Skin Removed
- Chipotle Sauce
- 1 Cup Mayonnaise
- ¼ Cup Extra-Virgin Olive Oil
- ½ Teaspoon Kosher or Sea Salt
- ¼ Teaspoon Freshly Ground Pepper
- ¼ Teaspoon Red Pepper Flakes
- 3 Tablespoons Buttermilk or Sour Cream
- 2 Canned Chipotle Chiles In Adobo Sauce, Minced

Instructions

- Prepare a medium-hot fire in a charcoal Traeger Grill or preheat a gas Traeger Grill on medium high. In a back   dish large enough to hold the halibut in a s le layer, combine the olive oil, ½ teaspoon salt, the pepper, and red pepper flakes. Stir to blend thoroughly. Add the halibut fillets and turn to coat on both sides. Set aside. While the Traeger Grill is heat, make the sauce: In a small bowl, combine the mayonnaise, buttermilk, chiles, cilantro, and ¼ teaspoon salt and mix well. Set aside. Oil the Traeger Grill grate.
- Use tongs to arrange the halibut fillets, flesh side down, directly over the medium-hot fire and cover. Traeger Grill the halibut until Traeger Grill marks

are etched across the fillets, about 3 minutes. Turn the fillets and re-cover the Traeger Grill.

- Cook until the halibut is almost opaque throughout but still very moist when tested with a knife, or an instant-read thermometer inserted in the center registers 125° to 130°F, 2 to 3 minutes longer. Us tongs or a spatula, transfer the fillets to warmed dinner plates, and accompany each fillet with a spoonful of the sauce. Serve immediately.

Tuna with a Black Tapenade Sauce
Ingredients

- 2 Tablespoons Kosher or Sea Salt
- Cup Coarsely Crushed Peppercorns
- 2 Tablespoons Extra-Virgin Olive Oil
- Cup Store-Bought Black Olive Tapenade
- 4 Ahi Tuna Steaks, 1¼ Inches Thick (About 5 Ounces Each)

Instructions

- Prepare a hot fire in a charcoal Traeger Grill or preheat a gas Traeger Grill on high. In a small bowl, combine the olive oil and tapenade and mix well. Set aside. On a dinner plate, mix together the salt and peppercorns and spread the mixture out on the plate.
- Press each tuna steak into the mixture, coat it heavily on both sides. Set aside on a separate plate. Oil the Traeger Grill grate. Use tongs to arrange the steaks directly over the hot fire. Traeger Grill the tuna until Traeger Grill marks are etched across the steaks, about 2 minutes. Turn the steaks and Traeger Grill until red-rare in the center when tested with a knife, or an instant read thermometer inserted in the center registers 120°F, about 2 minutes longer.
- Use tongs to transfer the steaks to a cut board and cut across the grain into ¼- inch-thick slices. Arrange the slices, overlap them, on warmed dinner plates, and accompany with a spoonful of the sauce. Serve immediately.

Spicy Tuna Steaks with Cayenne Pepper
Ingredients

- 3 Garlic Cloves Minced
- 3 Shallots Minced
- 2 Teaspoons Cayenne Pepper
- 2 Teaspoons Ground Cumin
- 6 Small Tuna Steaks (Weigh Around 170grams Each)
- 80ml Olive Oil
- 80ml Lemon Juice (Fresh Would Be Best)
- 4 Tablespoons Chopped Cilantro Leaves
- 1 Teaspoon Salt

Instructions

- In a bowl combine together well the lemon juice, olive oil, and 3 tablespoons of the cilantro leaves, garlic, shallots, cumin, cayenne pepper and salt. Now into a large resealable bag you place the tuna steaks and then pour the sauce you have just made over them.
- Make sure that you turn the bag over several times to ensure the sauce coats the steaks evenly then place in the refrigerator for 1 hour to allow them to marinate in the sauce. About 15 minutes before you remove the tuna steaks from the refrigerator you should start up your barbecue so it is heated up correctly for cook the steaks on it. Just before you take the steaks out of the marinade after remove from the refrigerator lightly oil the Traeger Grill on your barbecue and then place the tuna steaks on them.

- Make sure the Traeger Grill is placed as close to the heat source as possible as you need to cook the steaks on a high heat. You should cook each side of the tuna steaks for around 4 to 5 minutes or until you feel they are cooked to the way people enjoy eat this type of fish. Once they are cooked remove from the barbecue place on clean plates and sprinkle with the remain   cilantro and then serve.

Swordfish with Traeger Grilled Peppers and Olives

Ingredients

- Freshly Ground Pepper
- 2 Red Bell Peppers, Seeded, Defibbed, And Cut Lengthwise Into 6 Strips Each
- 2 Yellow Bell Peppers, Seeded, Defibbed, And Cut Lengthwise Into 6 Strips Each
- 4 Swordfish Fillets (6 To 7 Ounces Each), Skin Removed
- Tuscan Extra-Virgin Olive Oil
- Kosher or Sea Salt
- 1 Cup Pitted Sicilian-Style Green Olives, Quartered

Instructions

- Prepare a medium-hot fire in a charcoal Traeger Grill or preheat a gas Traeger Grill on medium high. Arrange the fillets on a rimmed back sheet and rub generously on both sides with olive oil. Sprinkle lightly on both sides with salt and pepper.
- Set aside. In a bowl, toss the peppers with olive oil to coat. Set aside. Oil the Traeger Grill grate. Use tongs to arrange the bell peppers directly over the medium hot fire and cook, turn once, until light Traeger Grill marks appear, about 2 minutes per side.
- Transfer to a warmed platter or rimmed back sheet and keep warm. Oil the Traeger Grill grate again. Use tongs to arrange the swordfish fillets directly over the medium-hot fire and cook, bast

frequently with olive oil, until Traeger Grill marks are etched across the fillets, about 3 minutes.

- Turn the fillets and cook, continue   to baste frequently, until almost opaque throughout but still very moist when tested with a knife, or an instant-read thermometer inserted in the center registers 125° to 130°F, about 3 minutes longer. Arrange a mixture of yellow and red peppers on each warmed dinner plate. Place a fillet on top, and scatter some olives over the fish. Serve immediately, with a drizzle of olive oil, if desired.

Grilled Shrimp with Soft Tacos and Salsa
Ingredients

- ¾ Cup Loosely Packed Fresh Cilantro Leaves
- 1 Large, Ripe Tomato, Cored, Halved Crosswise, Seeded, And Chopped
- 2 Cups Shredded Iceberg Lettuce
- 1 To 1½ Cups Store-Bought Salsa 8 8-Inch Flour Tortillas
- 2 Large Hass Avocados, Halved, Pitted, Peeled, And Cut into Thin Wedges
- 1 Pound Large Shrimp (26/30 Count), Peeled and Deveined, Tails Removed
- 2 Tablespoons Traeger Grill Every Day Spice Rub 1 Lime, Quartered

Instructions

- Prepare a medium-hot fire in a charcoal Traeger Grill or preheat a gas Traeger Grill on medium high. In a bowl, toss the shrimp with the spice rub until well coated. Arrange the lime, lettuce, cilantro, tomato, avocados, and salsa in separate small serve bowls and have them ready for assemble the tacos. Oil the Traeger Grill grate.
- Arrange the shrimp directly over the medium-hot fire and Traeger Grill, turn once, until the shrimp turn pink on the outside and are just opaque on the inside, about 2 minutes per side. While the shrimp are cook, Traeger Grill the tortillas.
- Depend on the size of the Traeger Grill, lay 1 or 2 tortillas on the Traeger Grill at a time, warm them over direct heat for about 15 seconds per side.

Stack them on a plate and keep warm. Transfer the shrimp to a serve   bowl. Let diners assemble their own tacos. To assemble, place 2 or 3 shrimp in a tortilla, squeeze a bit of lime juice over the shrimp, and mound lettuce, cilantro, tomato, and avocado on top. Finally, add a spoonful of salsa. Serve with plenty of napkins!

Grilled Salted Shrimp with Olive Oil
Ingredients

- ¼ Cup Loosely Packed Fresh Oregano Leaves
- ½ Cup Extra-Virgin Olive Oil
- 3 Large Cloves Garlic
- 1 Tablespoon Sea Salt
- 2 Pounds Large Shrimp (26/30 Count) In the Shell, Deveined

Instructions

- Prepare a medium-hot fire in a charcoal Traeger Grill or preheat a gas Traeger Grill on medium high. In a small food processor fitted with the metal blade, combine the garlic, salt, and oregano and process until minced. With the machine run, pour the olive oil through the feed tube and process until the marinade is well blended. Reserve 2 tablespoons of the marinade for bast. In a bowl, toss the shrimp with the remain marinade until well coated.
- Set aside while the Traeger Grill heats. Oil the Traeger Grill grate. Remove the shrimp from the marinade and arrange them directly over the medium-hot fire. Traeger Grill, turn once, until the shrimp turn pink on the outside and are just opaque on the inside, about 2 minutes per side. Baste the shrimp with the reserved marinade as they Traeger Grill. Transfer the shrimp to a serve bowl. Let diners peel their own shrimp and enjoy the fun of eat   with their f errs. Serve with plenty of napkins!

Traeger Grilled Sliced Calamari
Ingredients

- 1 Garlic Clove Thinly Sliced
- 2 Sprigs of Fresh Oregano or ½ Teaspoon Dried Oregano
- ½ Teaspoon Coarse Salt
- 450grams Fresh Calamari (Cleaned, Rinsed & Well Dried)
- 60ml Extra Virgin Olive Oil
- 1 ½ Tablespoons Fresh Lemon Juice (About 1 Small Lemon)
- Freshly Ground Black Pepper

Instructions

- In a bowl place the olive oil; lemon juice and salt then stir until they combined together. Then into this mix the garlic and the whole sprigs or dried oregano. Whilst you are making up this sauce you should be get the barbecue heated up and place the Traeger Grill down as low as possible in order to cook the calamari quick on a very high heat.
- When the barbecue has heated up place the squid on the oiled Traeger Grill and char each side of it for 1 minute. Now remove from the barbecue and slice all parts of the calamari include the tendrils cross wise into ¼ inch r s.
- Then add the calamari to the lemon sauce made earlier and then place on a serve plate. Just before you serve this dish to your guests make sure that you sprinkle over some freshly ground black pepper.

Large Grilled Shrimp Skewers
Ingredients

- 1 Teaspoon Soy Sauce
- 1 Teaspoon Vegetable Oil
- 2 Tablespoons Jamaican Jerk Season
- 3 Dashes Hot Pepper Sauce
- 900grams Large Shrimps (Peeled and Deveined)
- 80ml Fresh Lime Juice
- 80ml Honey
- Salt and Freshly Ground Black Pepper to Taste
- 12 Wooden Skewers That Have Been Soaked in Water for 1 Hour

Instructions

- In a bowl combine together the lime juice, honey, soy sauce and oil. Then to this add the Jamaican jerk season, hot pepper sauce, salt and pepper. Now add to the sauce you have just made the shrimps make sure that you mix everything well together so that the shrimps are completely coated in the sauce.
- Cover the bowl and place in the refrigerator and leave there for one hour to allow the shrimps to marinate in the sauce. This is the time when the skewers should have been placed in the water to soak. About 30 minutes before the shrimps are due to come out the refrigerator you should now get your barbecue go.
- The shrimps will need to be cooked on a medium to high heat so place the Traeger Grill of the barbecue about 4 to 6 inches above the heat

source. After remove   the shrimps from the refrigerator now remove the skewers from the water, then pat them dry before then spray   or brush   with some nonstick cook   spray or oil.

- Now thread on to each skewer the shrimps until all 12 skewers have been used and place on the Traeger Grill and cook each kebab for 5 minutes on each side or until the shrimps have turned pink in color. Once the shrimps are cooked place on clean plates and serve with the seasoned rice and frozen margaritas.

Tangy Shrimp with Garlic and Paprika
Ingredients

- 7 Tablespoons Lemon Juice (Fresh Would Be Ideal)
- 5 Tablespoons Worcestershire Sauce
- 28 Large Shrimps (Peeled & Deveined)
- 28 Large Sea Scallops
- 113grams Butter or Margarine
- 1 Teaspoon Garlic Powder
- 1 Teaspoon Paprika

Instructions

- In a large resealable bag place the scallops and shrimps. Now into a bowl (that can be used safely in a microwave) place the butter or margarine, the lemon juice, Worcestershire sauce, garlic powder and paprika. Cook on 50% power for about 1 to 1 ½ minutes or until the butter/margarine is melted then stir to ensure that all these Ingredients are blended together.
- Once the sauce is made set aside about a third of it as this you will then use to baste the shrimps and scallops in whilst they are cook. As for the rest of the sauce this must be poured over the scallops and shrimps in the bag. Meningeal the bag and turn it over several times to ensure that every scallop and shrimp is coated in the sauce and place in the refrigerator for one hour. Whilst in the refrigerator make sure that you turn the back over occasionally. Whilst the barbecue is heat up you can now prepare the kebabs.

- Take some wooden skewers that have been soak in water and thread alternately on to them the scallops and shrimps. Once all the kebabs are made place them on the preheated barbecue and cook them on a medium to hot heat for 6 minutes turn once during this time. Both before and during this cook   time baste them occasionally with the sauce you set to one side earlier. Then cook them for a further 8 to 10 minutes or longer until the shrimps have turned pink and the scallops opaque.

Traeger Grilled Oysters
  Ingredients

- Hot Sauce
- 12 to 18 Oysters for Each Person
- Melted Butter
- Worcestershire Sauce

Instructions

- Once the barbecue has heated up place the oysters on to the Traeger Grill on a medium to high heat. If you want to prevent any flare ups whilst the oysters are cook   as juices drip out of them then cover the Traeger Grill with some aluminum foil first.
- After place   the oysters on the Traeger Grill close the lid of the barbecue and let them cook. It is important that you keep a close eye on the oysters as they are cook. So, check them every 3 to 4 minutes.
- Once you notice the shells start   to open then remove them from the Traeger Grill. After remove the oysters from the Traeger Grill open the shells and then loosen the meat and place on a plate so your guests can then help themselves. Beside the plate of oysters put some bowls with the melted butter, hot sauce and Worcestershire sauce in them and which the guests can then spoon on top of the oysters if they wish. Then simply pop in the mouth and enjoy.

Thai Spiced Prawns
Ingredients

- 1 Tablespoon Dijon Mustard
- 2 Garlic Cloves Minced
- 1 Tablespoon Brown Sugar
- 450grams Medium Size Prawns (Peeled and Deveined)
- 3 Tablespoons Fresh Lemon Juice
- 1 Tablespoon Soy Sauce
- 2 Teaspoons Curry Paste

Instructions

- In either a resealable plastic bag or a shallow back dish mixes together the lemon juice, soy sauce, mustard, garlic, sugar and curry paste. Then add the prawns and mix all these Ingredients together thoroughly. Meningeal up the bag or cover the dish with some cl film and place in the refrigerator to marinate for 1 hour.
- Next heat up the barbecue and place the Traeger Grill down low as you will be cooking these prawns on a high heat. Once the barbecue is ready lightly oil the Traeger Grill and place the prawns that have been threaded onto skewers and cook on each side for 3 minutes each. If you want to make turn them over easier place the kebabs inside a fish basket. You will know when the prawns are ready, as they will turn a pink opaque color.
- As for the remain sauce, which you marinated the prawns in initially, transfer this to a small saucepan and heat up until it starts to boil. Allow it to boil for

a few minutes before then transfer to a bowl which your guests can then dip the kebabs in and which you have also used to baste the prawns in whilst cook.

Garlic Traeger Grilled Shrimps
Ingredients

- Salt to Taste
- 30ml Olive Oil
- 450grams Large Size Shrimps (Peeled and Deveined)
- 4 Garlic Cloves
- ¼ Teaspoon Freshly Ground Black Pepper to Taste

Instructions

- Start the barbecue up and lightly oil the Traeger Grill. Now take the four garlic cloves and chop them up then sprinkle with some salt and us   the back of a large knife smash the garlic up until it forms a paste. Then place the garlic with some olive oil in a fry   pan (skillet) and cook over a medium to low heat until the garlic starts to turn brown.
- This should take around 5 minutes then once the garlic has turned brown remove from heat. Next you take the shrimps and thread them onto wooden skewers and sprinkle over them some salt and pepper to season.
- Then brush one side of the shrimps with the garlic and olive oil mixture you made earlier and place this side down on to the barbecue. Cook the shrimps until they start to turn pink in color and they begin to curl. This should take around 4 minutes and then turn them over. But before place back down on the barbecue brush with more of the garlic oil and then cook for a further 4 minutes until

the flesh has turned opaque and the shrimps are
pink all over.

Traeger Grilled Oysters
Ingredients

- 1 Tablespoon Minced Shallots
- 1 Tablespoon Chopped Fennel Greens
- 24 Fresh Live Unopened Medium Size Oysters
- 1 Teaspoon Grounded Fennel Seed
- 226grams Softened Butter
- 1 Teaspoon Freshly Ground Black Pepper
- ½ Teaspoon Salt

Instructions

- Get the barbecue go so and place the Traeger Grill down low as possible as you will be cooking the oysters on a very high heat. In a bowl mix together the butter, fennel seeds, shallots, fennel greens, pepper and salt.
- Then put to one side for use later. If you want place in the refrigerator to keep the butter from melt completely and remove about 10 minutes before needed. Place the oysters on the Traeger Grill of the barbecue and close the lid and leave it closed for between 3 and 5 minutes or until you start to hear them hiss or they start to open.
- Take an oyster knife and pry each one of the oysters open at the h e and loosen the oyster inside. Discard the flat part of the shell and then top each of the open oysters with ½ teaspoon of the butter you made earlier and then return them back to the barbecue once more. Then cook them once more until the butter has melted and is hot.

Traeger Grilled Crab with Minced Cilantro
Ingredients

- 1 Tablespoon Freshly Minced Ginger
- 1 Jalapeno Chili Seeds Removed Then Minced
- 1 Tablespoon Minced Cilantro
- 2 Large Live Crabs
- 60ml White Wine Vinegar
- 2 ½ Teaspoons Sugar
- 2 Tablespoons Olive Oil
- 1 Medium Tomato Chopped

Instructions

- In a bowl mix together the chopped tomato, vinegar, oil, Ginger, chili, garlic and cilantro. Then place to one side for use later. Now into a large pot of boil water place the crabs one at the time head first. Reduce the heat and allow the crabs to sit in simmer water for 5 minutes before then remove. If, however you find the thought of cook live crabs a little too much then you can use frozen ones instead. Of course, you need to allow them sufficient time to thaw out before you can start cook with them.
- After remove the crabs from the water turn over and pull the triangular tab from the belly and lift of the shell. Remove the entrails and gills from the crab before then wash and drain. Now place on the barbecue that you have preheated and close the lid. But before clos the lid brush with the mixture you made earlier and do this regularly

throughout the time the crabs are Traeger Grill on the barbecue.

- About halfway through the cook   time (around about 5minutes) you need to turn the crabs over and repeat the same process again for a further 5 minutes or until the meat in the legs of the crabs has turned opaque.
- Now place the crabs on to a plate to serve them but before you do serve spoon over any remain sauce you have that you used to baste the crabs in when cook. If you wish you can put the meat back in the shells before serve.

Sesame Scallops with Vegetable Oil
Ingredients

- 2 Tablespoons Soy Sauce
- 2 Tablespoons Dry Sherry
- 1 Tablespoon Freshly Minced Ginger
- 1 Teaspoon Sesame Oil
- 1 Garlic Clove Minced
- 1 Green Onion Minced
- Sesame Seeds
- 900grams Fresh Sea Scallops
- 60ml Vegetable Oil
- 60ml Distilled White Vinegar
- 2 Tablespoons Hoisin Sauce

Instructions

- First off wash and then pat dry with some paper towels the scallops. Now into a bowl mix together the oil, vinegar, hoisin and soy sauce, dry sherry, Ginger, sesame oil, garlic and onion. Then pour this mixture into a resealable bag and then add to these the scallops. Turn the bag over several times to ensure that all the scallops are covered in the marinade and place in the refrigerator overnight.
- Whilst the barbecue is heat   up you can now remove the scallops from the refrigerator and thread them on to skewers ready for cook. Once placed on the skewers then sprinkle over some of the sesame seeds and cook over a medium heat (so place the Traeger Grill about 4 to 6 inches above the heat source) and cook for 6 to 8 minutes.

You will know the scallops are ready to eat when they have turned opaque.

Margarita Shrimps with Olive Oil
Ingredients

- 3 Tablespoons Olive Oil
- ¼ Teaspoon Ground Red Pepper
- ¼ Teaspoon Salt
- 2 Teaspoons Tequila
- 3 Tablespoons Freshly Chopped Cilantro
- 450grams Shrimps (Peeled and Deveined)
- 2 Garlic Cloves Minced
- 2 Tablespoons Fresh Lime Juice

Instructions

- In a bowl place the lime juice, olive oil, tequila, garlic, cilantro, pepper and salt and combine well together before then add   the shrimps. Toss the mixture about lightly to ensure that the shrimps are covered in the sauce then cover the bowl and place in the refrigerator for between 30 minutes and 3 hours to marinate.
- Turn on or light the barbecue about 30 minutes prior to when you want to start cook   the shrimps. You need to place the Traeger Grill down low in the barbecue, as you will be cook   these on a high heat for a very short space of time. Whilst the barbecue is heat   up take the shrimps out of the fridge and thread them on to either metal or wooden skewers. Put about 3 or 4 on each skewer and place to one side. If there is any marinade left over in the bowl discard this. Before you place the shrimps on to the barbecue Traeger Grill lightly oil it first to prevent the shrimps from stick to it.

- Now cook the shrimps for between 2 and 3 minutes on each side or until they have turned pink. Then serve.

Scallops with An Oregano Leaves
Ingredients

- 32grams Fresh Thyme Leaves
- 3 Garlic Cloves Chopped
- 2 Teaspoons Chicken Flavored Bouillon Granules
- 1 Teaspoon Freshly Shredded Lemon Peel
- 450grams Scallops (About 12 to 15 Scallops)
- 64grams Toasted Pecan Pieces
- 43grams Fresh Oregano Leaves
- ¼ Teaspoon Freshly Ground Black Pepper
- 3 Tablespoons Olive Oil

Instructions

- In a food processor place the pecan pieces, oregano, thyme, garlic, bouillon granules, lemon peel and black pepper. Turn machine on until they form a paste then very slowly and gradually add the olive oil. Once you have formed a paste now rub it onto the scallops and then thread three of each on to a skewer. If you are us wooden ones remember to soak in water for at least 30 minutes to prevent them from burn when on the barbecue.
- Once the scallops are ready on the skewers place on the preheated barbecue over a medium heat so set the Traeger Grill about 6 inches above the heat source and cook them for between 5 and 8 minutes.
- The best way of know when the scallops are ready to serve is to see if they have turned opaque in color. As soon as the scallops are cooked serve to your guests on clean plates with some crusty bread

and a crisp green salad that has been drizzled with lemon juice and olive oil.

Grilled Scallops & Tomato Kebabs
Ingredients

- 2 Tablespoons Olive Oil
- 2 Tablespoons Dijon Mustard
- 1/8 Teaspoon Salt
- 16 Large Sea Scallops
- 24 Cherry Tomatoes
- 1 Lemon

Instructions

- Start prepare   the barbecue for cook   this dish on a medium heat. This means putt   the Traeger Grill of the barbecue about 6 inches above the main heat source. Also place the wooden skewers in some water. Whilst the barbecue is heat   up you can now prepare the sauce for the kebabs. In a bowl place 1 tablespoon of lemon juice along with ½ teaspoon of its peel. To this then add the olive oil, Dijon mustard and salt and mix well together. Then put to one side ready for use later.
- Now on to each of the wooden skewers you need to thread 3 tomatoes and 2 scallops alternately. You should start and finish with the tomatoes. Next brush the kebabs you have just made with some of the sauce you made earlier and place on the barbecue to cook. Each kebab will need to cook for between 7 and 9 minutes and should be turned over several times. After this time has elapsed brush the kebabs with the remainder of the sauce and then cook for another 5 minutes or more remember   to turn them over frequently. The

kebabs will be ready to consume when the scallops have turned opaque right through.

- Once the kebabs are cooked served to your guests immediately with a little green salad and some crusty bread.

Traeger Grilled Lobster with Butter
Ingredients

- 60ml Fresh Lime Juice
- ½ Teaspoon Crushed Bay Leaf
- ¼ Teaspoon Freshly Ground Black Pepper
- 3 x 680grams Fresh Lobsters
- 113grams Butter
- ¼ Teaspoon Salt

Instructions

- To parboil the lobsters, you need to bra   around 3 inches of water to boil in an 8-quart saucepan. Once the water begins boil   add the lobsters, then cover the pan and cook for 10 minutes. Once the 10 minutes has elapsed remove the lobsters from the pan and leave them to one side to cool. Whilst the barbecue is heat   up in another saucepan place the butter, lime juice, bay leaf, salt and pepper and cook for 10 minutes over a low heat. Then put to one side to use later on.
- By now the lobsters should have cooled down sufficiently to enable you to cut them in half lengthwise and brush them with the butter mixture you have just made. After brush   the cut side of the lobster with the butter mixture you place them cut side down onto the Traeger Grill of the barbecue which you have placed about 4 inches above the heat source and cook them for 5 minutes.
- Now turn the lobsters over carefully brush   them with some more of the butter mixture and continue

cook   them on the barbecue until the meat is cooked through. This should take about another 5 minutes. As soon as the meat is cooked through remove the lobsters from the barbecue place on a clean plate and garnish them with lime wedges and bay leaves if you want. Each of your guests should be given ½ lobster each.

Traeger Grilled Prawns & Garlic Chili Sauce
Ingredients

- 5 Fresh Thai Chili's Thinly Sliced
- 1 Shallot Thinly Sliced
- 2 Kaffir Lime Leaves
- 1 Tablespoon Fish Sauce
- 450grams Jumbo Size Prawns (Devein Them)
- 2 Tablespoons Cook   Oil
- 2 Tablespoons Minced Garlic
- 2 Tablespoons Thinly Sliced Lemon Grass
- Juice Of 1 Lime
- 1 Tablespoon Thai Roasted Chili Paste
- 1 Tablespoon Torn Fresh Mint Leaves

Instructions

- Turn on or light your barbecue ready for cook   the prawns on. Place   the Traeger Grill which has been lightly oiled about 6 inches above the heat sauce allow   you to cook the prawns on a medium heat. Once the barbecue is heated up now place the prawns on to the Traeger Grill and cook until the outside starts to turn pink and the meat inside no longer looks transparent. They will need to cook for between 5 and 10 minutes and should be turned over frequently. Whilst they are cook   you should now be making   the sauce, which the prawns can then be dipped into. To make the sauce heat some oil over a medium heat in a skillet and to this then add the garlic until it turns brown, which should take around 7 to 10 minutes.

- Now remove from the heat and to the oil and garlic add the lemon grass, chilies, shallot, lime leaves, fish sauce, lime juice and chili paste. Toss to combine all these Ingredients together then spoon some of them over the prawns, which you have removed from the barbecue and placed on a serve dish and the rest you pour into a bowl. Garnish with the freshly torn mint leaves.

Traeger Grilled New England Seafood
Ingredients

- 225grams Red New Potatoes (Skins Scrubbed then Thinly Sliced)
- 2 Ears of Corn Quartered
- 2 Tablespoons Butter (Room Temperature)
- 2 Tablespoons Finely Chopped Fresh Dill
- 1 Small Garlic Clove Minced
- 450grams Skinless Cod Fillet (Cut into Four Equal Pieces)
- 225grams Frozen Uncooked Prawns (Peeled and Deveined and Thawed)
- Coarse Salt and Freshly Ground Black Pepper to Taste
- 1 Lemon Thinly Sliced

Instructions

- Start by get your barbecue go and place the Traeger Grill 6 inches above the heat source to allow the packets you are about to make to cook on a medium heat. Whilst the barbecue is heat up in a bowl mix together the butter, dill, garlic, salt and pepper and place to one side for now. Take four squares of aluminum foil measure 14 inches square each. On to each of these four pieces of foil first place the thinly sliced potatoes before then place on top of them a piece of the cod.
- Next lay on some of the prawns and alongside the potatoes; cod and prawns place two pieces of the corn. Season each parcel with salt and pepper before add a spoonful of the butter mixture on

64

top. Then place on top of these two slices of the lemon. Now bra   up the sides of the foil and crimp the edges to seal the   Ingredients inside them tightly. Place each parcel on to the Traeger Grill make   sure that the potato is on the bottom and cook for about 12 to 14 minutes or until the fish is just cooked through and the potatoes are tender. You should make sure that you rotate not flip the parcels occasionally as this will help to ensure that everything   inside is cooked properly. Once the cook   time has passed remove the parcels from the heat and slit open the top of each one and transfer the contents to plates. If you want garnish the food with some more dill sprigs and serve some warm crusty rolls with them.

Honey Traeger Grilled Shrimps
Ingredients

- 80ml Worcestershire Sauce
- 2 Tablespoons Dry White Wine
- 57grams Melted Butter
- 2 Tablespoons Worcestershire Sauce
- 2 Tablespoons Italian Style Salad Dress
- Honey Sauce
- 450grams Large Shrimps
- ½ Teaspoon Garlic Powder
- ¼ Tablespoon Freshly Ground Black Pepper
- 60ml Honey

Instructions

- Into a large bowl mix together the garlic powder, black pepper, Worcestershire sauce, dry white wine and the salad dress. Then add the shrimp and toss them to coat them evenly in the marinade. Now cover the bowl over and place in the refrigerator to let the shrimp marinate in the sauce for 1 hour.
- Start the barbecue up and place the Traeger Grill, which needs to be lightly, oiled about 4 inches above the heat source to allow the shrimps to cook on a high heat. Remove the shrimps from the marinade and thread onto skewers. Pierce one through the head then the next one through the tail. Any marinade left over can now be discarded. Then set the shrimps to one side for a moment whilst you make the honey sauce. To make the honey sauce in a small bowl mix together the honey melted butter and the other 2 tablespoons

of Worcestershire sauce. This is what you will be bast   the shrimps in as they cook.

- Take the shrimps and place on the lightly oiled Traeger Grill and cook for 2 to 3 minutes on each side, make   sure you baste them occasionally with the honey sauce you have just made. You will know when the shrimps are ready to serve because the flesh will have turned opaque throughout. Serve to your guests immediately once cooked.

Grilled Scallops Wrapped in Prosciutto
Ingredients

- 2 Lemons Halved
- Freshly Ground Black Pepper
- Extra Virgin Olive Oil (For Drizzle)
- 900grams (40) Medium Sized Scallops
- 450grams Paper Thin Slices Prosciutto

Instructions

- Turn your gas barbecue on to high and allow to heat up whilst you are preparing the scallops for cook. If you are us a charcoal barbecue you will know when it is hot enough when you can only hold your hand over it about 5 inches above the Traeger Grill for 2 seconds. Take one slice of the prosciutto and cut in half lengthwise then fold in half and wrap it around the sides of a scallop. You need to make sure that the ends of the prosciutto overlap and then thread it on to a skewer. Do the same for the other pieces of prosciutto and the scallops. Next take the olive oil and drizzle it lightly over the scallops and then squeeze some lemon juice over them. Then season with the freshly ground black pepper.
- Then place on the barbecue to cook. Cook on each side for about 3 minutes or until you see the flesh of the scallops has turned opaque. Remove from barbecue place on a clean plate with some lemon wedges and serve to your guests.

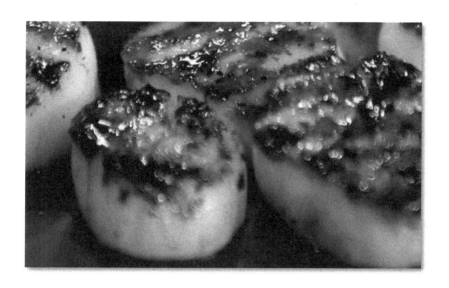

Shrimp & Scallop Kebabs
Ingredients

- ½ Teaspoon Salt
- ½ Teaspoon Freshly Ground Black Pepper
- 120ml Tomato Ketchup
- 60ml Orange Juice
- 60ml Maple Syrup
- ½ Teaspoon Paprika
- 3 Garlic Cloves Minced
- 12 Jumbo Shrimps (Peeled and Deveined)
- 12 Large Sea Scallops
- 3 Tablespoons Vegetable Oil
- 1 Tablespoon Worcestershire Sauce
- 1 Tablespoon Apple Cider Vinegar

Instructions

- Onto a skewer thread 3 scallops and 3 shrimps alternately. Then brush with the vegetable before season with the salt and pepper. Then place to one side for cook later. In to bowl put the ketchup, orange juice, maple syrup, Worcestershire sauce, apple cider vinegar, paprika and garlic and combine well together.
- This you will then be used for bast the scallops and shrimps as they cook on the barbecue. So, set to onside until you start cook. Whilst you are do the various tasks above you should be get your barbecue started with the Traeger Grill be set about 4 to 6 inches above the heat source so the food can cook on a medium to high heat.

- As soon as your barbecue is ready lightly oil the Traeger Grill and then place the shrimp and scallop kebabs on it. But just before you do brush the kebabs all over with the maple orange sauce and then baste them with it regularly. Each side of these kebabs should be allowed to cook for 2 to 3 minutes or until the flesh of the scallops and shrimps have turned opaque.

Black Pepper Ginger Shrimp

- **Ingredients**
- 3 Tablespoons Vegetable Oil
- 4 Ripe Plum Tomatoes (Cut in Half Lengthwise)
- 1 Teaspoon Sugar
- 1 Tablespoon Freshly Chopped Cilantro
- 1 Tablespoon Freshly Chopped Basil
- 2 Medium Green Tomatoes (Cut in Half Lengthwise)
- Coarse Salt
- Freshly Ground Black Pepper
- 2 Tablespoons Fresh Lime Juice
- 20 Extra Large Shrimps (Peeled, Deveined but Tails Left On)
- 2 Garlic Cloves Minced
- 1 ½ Tablespoons Grated Peeled Ginger
- 1 Tablespoon Freshly Minced Jalapeno Chili (With Seeds)

Instructions

- In to a bowl mix together the garlic and Ginger. Now take half of this and transfer to another bowl and add to these 2 tablespoons of the oil before then add the shrimps and toss them in the mixture to make sure that they are evenly coated in it.
- Now cover this bowl over and place in the refrigerator for 30 minutes to allow the shrimps to marinate. As for the rest of the Ginger and garlic mixture this should be covered and placed in the refrigerator as well. Now heat up the barbecue and

whilst this is happening   into another bowl put the tomatoes and toss them in the last tablespoon of oil along with some salt and pepper to season. Now Traeger Grill the tomatoes on the barbecue the cut sides fac   upwards until the skins become charred and the flesh inside becomes tender.

- The plum tomatoes will take around 4 to 6 minutes to cook and the green tomatoes will take about 8 to 10 minutes to cook. If the green tomatoes are especially hard, they may need a little longer than 10 minutes.

- Also be careful when cook   the tomatoes as both the juices from them and the oil in which they are coated may cause flare ups to occur. Once the skins have become charred on the tomatoes and the flesh soft remove from heat and set to one side to allow them to cool down a little. As soon as they have cooled down enough peel away and discard the skins and seeds then finely chop them up and add to the garlic and Ginger mixture from earlier. Also add to this mixture the lime juice, jalapeno chili, sugar cilantro and basil then well combined together pour into a serve   dish and set to one side for later.

- Remove shrimps from refrigerator and just before place   on to the barbecue thread one shrimp on to a skewer through both the top and tail and sprinkle with some salt and pepper. Place on the barbecue and cook for about 2 minutes on each side or until the flesh has turned opaque throughout. Once cooked place the skewers on to a clean plate along with the bowl of tomato relish you made earlier.

Traeger Grilled Crab Legs
Ingredients

- 2 Tablespoons Olive Oil
- 450grams K   Crab Legs per Person
- 2 Tablespoons Melted Butter

Instructions

- Preheat the barbecue and place the Traeger Grill around 6 inches above the heat source as the crab's legs will need to be cooked on a medium heat. Whilst the barbecue is heat   up in a bowl mix together the olive oil and butter and then brush this over the crab legs. Now place the crab legs on the Traeger Grill, which you may want to lightly oil as well and close the lid on your barbecue.
- Now let the legs cook on the barbecue for between 4 and 5 minutes make   sure that halfway through you turn them over.
- Once the crab legs are cooked remove from the barbecue and serve them with some fresh crusty bread along with a cocktail or garlic butter sauce. To make the garlic butter sauce in a sauce pan place 50grams of melted butter with 1 tablespoon of freshly chopped garlic and heat gently. Do   this will then allow the flavor of the garlic to become infused in the butter.

Grilled Shrimp & Broccoli Florets
Ingredients

- 225grams Medium Size Shrimps (Peeled and Deveined)
- 175grams Instant Rice
- 2 Teaspoons Seafood Season
- 2 Garlic Cloves Minced
- 220grams Broccoli Florets
- 2 Tablespoons Butter (Cut into Pieces)
- 8 Ice Cubes
- 120ml Water

Instructions

- Preheat the barbecue and place the Traeger Grill about 4 to 6 inches above the heat source so you can cook these parcels on a medium to high heat. Whilst the barbecue is heat up place half the shrimps on a piece of aluminum foil with the nonstick (dull) side fac up towards the food.
- Then around this arrange half the rice and sprinkle it and the shrimps with some of the seafood season before then top off the shrimps with half the minced garlic. Then place half the broccoli on top of the shrimp and sprinkle with garlic and butter. Do the same for the other parcel and then top each one off with 4 ice cubes. Now bra the sides of the aluminum foil up and double fold over the top and at one end. At the end, which is still open, pour in half the water and then fold this end over so that the Ingredients are congealed inside.

- Make sure that you use a large enough piece of foil to allow room for heat and steam to circulate inside. Once the parcels are ready place on the barbecue and let them cook for 9 to 13 minutes. It is important that you close the lid whilst the parcels are cook   to ensure that the s cook evenly. After remove   from the Traeger Grill snip open the parcels and stir the rice before you then serve as they are to your guests. It is also a good idea to squeeze some fresh lemon juice over the shrimps, rice and broccoli just before serve.

Barbecued Oysters Served with Rice Vinegar
Ingredients

- 2 Finely Chopped Shallots
- 3 Tablespoons Freshly Squeezed (Strained) Lime Juice
- 1 Small Jalapeno Chili (Seeded and Finely Chopped)
- 48 Oysters (Scrubbed)
- Hogwash
- 120ml Natural Rice Vinegar
- 120ml Seasoned Rice Vinegar
- Fresh Roughly Chopped Cilantro

Instructions

- Heat up the barbecue until it is very hot then place the unopened fresh oysters on to the lightly oiled Traeger Grill and close the lid. After about 3 minutes check to see if the oysters are open. If the oysters are open then detach the oysters from the top shell us   an oyster knife.
- Then loosen the top shells and discard these. Then you simply need to place a spoonful of the Hogwash sauce you have made over each one before serve them. In order to make the Hogwash place the seasoned and natural rice vinegar into a bowl with the shallots, lime juice, jalapeno chili and cilantro and mix well together.
- You should make this before you actually begin cook   the oysters, as it needs to go into the refrigerator for at least an hour.

Black Pepper Scallops, Orange & Cucumber Kebabs

Ingredients

- 120ml Fresh Orange Juice
- 8 Very Thin Slices Peeled Fresh Ginger
- 2 Tablespoons Honey
- Freshly Ground Black Pepper
- ½ Navel Orange Cut into Wedges
- ½ Cucumber Cut in Half Lengthways Then Cut Into ½ Inch Slices
- Coarse Salt
- 450grams Large Scallops

Instructions

- Start by get the barbecue heated up. You will need to place the lightly oiled Traeger Grill about 6 inches above the heat source as you want to cook these kebabs on a medium heat to ensure that north burns.
- Whilst the barbecue is heat up in a small bowl mix together the honey and orange juice and set to one side for later. Next take four skewers (wooden ones will do but you can use metal ones if you want). On to these threads an orange wedge followed by a slice of Ginger, cucumber and scallop until each skewer is full.
- Also make sure that you end with another wedge of orange on the kebabs. Nonseason each kebab with salt and pepper before then brush with the orange and honey sauce made earlier. Place each kebab on to the Traeger Grill of the barbecue and

cook for between 4 and 6 minutes or until the scallop flesh has turned opaque.

- Make sure that you turn the kebabs frequently and baste regularly with the sauce. Once the kebabs are cooked serve with some rice or a crisp green salad.

Prawns with Pictou Virgin Olive Oil
Ingredients

- 12 Anchovy Fillets (Rinsed)
- 2 Garlic Cloves (Peeled)
- 60ml Extra Virgin Olive Oil
- Coarse Salt
- Freshly Ground Black Pepper
- 12 Prawns (Shelled and Deveined but With Heads Left On)
- 27.5grams Whole Raw Almonds
- 128grams Loose Packed Fresh Flat Leaf Parsley
- 2 Tablespoons Extra Virgin Olive Oil
- Zest of 1 Lemon

Instructions

- Take the whole raw almonds and place in the oven on a back   tray for 10 minutes at 350 degrees Fahrenheit. Stir the almonds occasionally and remove from oven when golden brown and fragrant. Then allow to cool down completely before coarsely chop them. Now take the coarsely chopped almonds and place them in food processor with the basil, parsley, anchovies and garlic and process until all have been combined together. Then to this paste add the oil very slowly in a steady stream and continue process   until a smooth paste is formed. Now transfer this mixture to a large bowl and mix in the lemon zest, salt and pepper. Put around a ¼ of this mixture to one side, as this is what your guests will then dip the shrimps in after they are cooked.

- Whilst you are preparing the Pictou you should be allow the barbecue to heat up ready for cook. Place the Traeger Grill about 5 inches above the heat source, as you will want to cook the shrimps on a medium to high heat. As soon as the barbecue is ready toss the shrimps in the rest of the Pictou and place them o
- n the barbecue and cook for about 2 ½ minutes on each side. Plus, before place on the barbecue season with some salt and pepper. You should only turn the shrimps over once during the cook time and to make sure that they are cooked through the flesh should be firm and they should have turned pink. As soon as the shrimps are cooked place onto a clean plate with some lemon wedges and the bowl of Pictou you put to one side earlier. Your guests can then dip the shrimps into this.

Grilled Black & White Pepper Shrimps
Ingredients

- 1 ½ Tablespoons Maldon Sea Salt
- 3 Tablespoons Safflower Oil
- 8 Sprigs Fresh Cilantro for Garnish
- 450grams Jumbo Shrimps (Heads Still on But Peeled & Deveined)
- 1 Tablespoon Black Peppercorns
- 2 Teaspoons White Peppercorns

Instructions

- In a shallow dish place 8 wooden skewers measure 10 inches in cold water for at least 10 minutes.

Nienstedt the barbecue up putts the Traeger Grill about 6 inches above the heat source so that the shrimps can cook on a medium to high heat. Whilst the barbecue is heat up thread the shrimps on to the skewers start with at the tail and thread through the body until it comes out of the head. Now put each one of these on to a back tray for now. In a mortar place the peppercorns and coarsely grind them together with a pestle.

- Then transfer these to a small bowl and mix into them the sea salt. Just before you place the shrimps on the barbecue drizzle them with the oil (both sides) and then sprinkle with the peppercorn and salt mixture. Now place the shrimps on the lightly oiled barbecue Traeger Grill and cook until the prawns become a light pink color and slightly charred. This should take around 2 minutes to occur then turn the shrimps over and cook for about the same amount of time again. To serve place the shrimps on a place and sprinkle with the sprigs of cilantro and a dip sauce in a bowl.

Traeger Grilled Prawns

 Ingredients

- ¼ Tablespoon Freshly Chopped Cilantro
- 1 Thai or Serrano Chili Minced
- 180ml Peanut or Canola Oil
- Vinaigrette
- 60ml Lime Juice
- 900grams (16-20) Extra Large Shrimps
- 32grams Minced Lemon Grass (White Part Only)
- 2 Tablespoons Cold Water
- 3 Tablespoons Grated Lime Zest
- 1 Tablespoon Freshly Minced Ginger Root
- 32grams Fresh Minced Ginger Root
- 2 Tablespoons Minced Garlic
- 60ml Rice Wine Vinegar
- 120ml Japanese Sweet Wine (Mirin)
- 2 Tablespoons Dark Soy Sauce
- 2 Teaspoons Fish Sauce
- 2 Fresh Thai or Serrano Chili's (Seeds Removed)
- 2 Teaspoons Minced Garlic
- 113grams Unsalted Smooth Peanut Butter

Instructions

- In a bowl (large) combine together the Ginger, lemon grass, garlic, cilantro, chili and oil. Then add the shrimps and let them marinate in the sauce made for 20 to 30 minutes at room temperature. Whilst the shrimps are marina in the sauce you can nonintact heat up the barbecue place the Traeger Grill about 6 inches above the heat source.

- This will then enable you to cook the shrimps that you will thread on to skewers on a medium to high heat. Now into a food processor place the lime juice, rice vinegar, mirin, soy sauce and water and blend.
- Then add to this the lime zest, Ginger, fish sauce, chilies, garlic and peanut butter and process until the mixture becomes smooth.
- Whilst these Ingredients are combining together slowly pour in the peanut oil until the mixture looks smooth and creamy. Pour this mixture into a bowl and then stir into it the mint, cilantro and chopped peanuts. Add some salt if needed. To cook the shrimps remove them from the marinade, shake off any excess and thread them on to skewers then cook them on either side for about 2 minutes or until they have turned pink and firm. Once cooked serve on a plate immediately with the sauce beside them.

Traeger Grilled Rock Lobster
Ingredients

- 1 Tablespoon Freshly Squeezed Lemon Juice
- 1 Tablespoon Olive Oil
- ½ Teaspoon Dried Oregano
- ¼ Teaspoon Salt
- 6 x 226gram Rock or Spiny Lobster Tails
- 12 Green Onions
- 1 Tablespoon Grated Orange Rind
- 2 Tablespoons Freshly Squeezed Orange Juice
- Dash of Hot Sauce (Such as Cholula)
- 1 Garlic Clove Minced
- 2 Tablespoons Melted Butter

Instructions

- Get the barbecue go so it is ready in time for cook to begin. Now you need to start prepare the lobster. To do this cut each lobster tail in half lengthwise and then coat each one along with the onions with some cook spray. Next place the tails on to the Traeger Grill of the barbecue cut side fac downwards and after you have oiled the Traeger Grill lightly.
- Traeger Grill the tails for 3 minutes and then turn them over. Now Traeger Grill them for a further five minutes.
- About 2 minutes after turn over the tails now place the green onions on the Traeger Grill to cook. These will require about 3 minutes and should be turned over at least once during this cook time.

- Remove from barbecue once they have become tender. To make the sauce which you will serve with the lobster tails in to a bowl place the orange rind, orange juice, lime juice, olive oil, oregano, salt, hot sauce and garlic and whisk well.
- Then very gradually add to this mixture the melted butter makes sure that you whisk the Ingredients continuously then drizzle it over the cut side of the tails. Transfer to a clean plate and serve alongside them some warm tortillas and some lime wedges.

Grilled Bacon Wrapped Shrimps
Ingredients

- Barbecue Seasoning to Taste
- 16 Large Shrimps (Peeled and Deveined)
- 8 Slices of Bacons

Instructions

- Preheat the barbecue and place the Traeger Grill about 4 to 6 inches above the heat. Take each shrimp and wrap them in half of each slice of bacon and then secure with a toothpick or thread two of them on to a wooden skewer that has been soak in water for 30 minutes. Nonwinged some of the season over them and then place each one on to the lightly oiled barbecue Traeger Grill and cook for around 10 to 15 minutes.
- It is important that you turn the shrimps over frequently to prevent the bacon from burn and also to ensure that the shrimps are cooked through evenly. Once cooked place on a clean plate and allow your guests to help themselves.

Salted Asparagus Spears
Ingredients

- Kosher or Sea Salt
- 28 Thick Asparagus Spears
- 1 To 2 Tablespoons Extra-Virgin Olive Oil
- Freshly Ground Pepper

Instructions

- Preheat a gas Traeger Grill on top. Snap off the fibrous bottom end of every and every spear, or cut the entire bunch into a uniform length. If wanted, us a vegetable peeler or sharp level knife, peel off the thick spears from marginally under the tip to the foundation. (This is not an important thing; many cooks prefer their own asparagus peeled, whereas some others enjoy them) Put the spears at a back dish, then toss them together with the olive oil, and season lightly with salt and pepper. Oil that the Traeger Grill grate.
- Put the asparagus straight over the hot flame and Traeger Grill, flip a couple days, till Traeger Grill marks show up on either side and the spears are crisp-tender, about 4 minutes. (Tim will change depend on the depth of their spears.) Transfer to a heated platter and serve immediately.

Grilled Corn in the Husk
Ingredients

- Unsalted Butter, At Room Temperature
- 4 Ears of Corn, Husks Intact
- Kosher or Sea Salt (Optional) Freshly Ground Pepper (Optional)

Instructions

- Preheat a gas Traeger Grill on top. Pull back the husk from every ear of corn with no really remove it. Eliminate the silk, then re-cover the corn with the husk. Run water into the ears of corn, then drain the surplus, then twist on the husks in the very top to close. Oil that the Traeger Grill grate.
- Set the corn straight over the hot flame and Traeger Grill, flip the ears a couple occasions to Traeger Grill on all sides, until the husks are charred and the kernels are tender and gently burnished, about 20 minutes. Eliminate from the Traeger Grill and pull and drop the husks, or knot the dragged back husks to get a rustic-chic appearance. Generously brush the corn with butter and season with pepper and salt, if needed. Transfer to a heated platter and serve hot.

Grilled Walla Walla Sweet Onions
Ingredients

- Cup Canola or Grapeseed Oil
- ¾ Teaspoon Ground Chipotle Chile
- 2 Large Walla Walla Or Other Sweet Onions, Cut Crosswise Into ½-Inch-Thick Slices

- ½ Teaspoon Kosher or Sea Salt

Instructions

- Preheat a gas Traeger Grill on top. Arrange the onion slices at a le coating on a large, rimmed rear sheet. In a small bowl, combine the oil, chile, and salt and blend well. Brush both sides of each onion piece with the oil. O
- il that the Traeger Grill grate. Set the onions right over the hot flame and Traeger Grill, turn after, till Traeger Grill marks look on either side along with the onions are crisp-tender, about 4 minutes each side. (Use a combo of tongs and a long-handled spatula to flip the onion pieces in order that they remain intact.) Transfer to a heated platter and serve hot, or keep warm until ready to serve.

Traeger Grilled Roma Tomatoes
Ingredients

- 1 Teaspoon Minced Garlic
- ¼ Teaspoon Kosher or Sea Salt
- 8 4-Inch-Long Sprigs Fresh Rosemary
- 2 Tablespoons Roasted Garlic-Flavored Olive Oil, Plus More for Brush
- 2 Teaspoons Minced Fresh Basil
- ¼ Teaspoon Freshly Ground Pepper
- 4 Roma Tomatoes, Halved Crosswise

Instructions

- Run water on the rosemary sprigs to soften them. Put aside. In a small bowl, combine the 2 tablespoons garlic-flavored olive oil, basil, salt, garlic, and pepper. Put aside. Arrange the tomatoes, cut side up, on a rimmed back sheet or a plate and brush the cut side of each tomato with the olive oil mix.
- Oil that the Traeger Grill grate. Organize the lavender sprigs in a row, then vertical to the pubs of this Traeger Grill grate and marginally split, directly above the moderate flame. Put the tomatoes, cut side down, on top of the rosemary. Us tongs, gently turn the tomatoes cut side up, and brush off some of those charred rosemary leaves. Brush the tomatoes liberally using the olive oil mix. Cover and Traeger Grill till the berries are hot and tender but still hold their shape, about two minutes more. Transfer to a heated serve platter or dinner

plates and serve immediately, or keep warm until ready to serve.

Traeger Grilled of Zucchini
Ingredients

- 3 Pattypan Or Other Yellowing Summer Squashes, Ends Trimmed and Cut into Thick
- Slices (See Headnote) 3 Zucchini, Ends Trimmed and Cut on The Diagonal Into
- Thick Slices
- 2 Tablespoons Store-Bought Basil Pesto
- 3 Tablespoons Extra-Virgin Olive Oil, Plus More for Brush
- Kosher or Sea Salt
- Freshly Ground Pepper

Instructions

- Run water on the rosemary sprigs to soften them. Put aside. In a small bowl, combine the 2 tablespoons garlic-flavored olive oil, basil, salt, garlic, and pepper. Put aside. Arrange the tomatoes, cut side up, on a rimmed back sheet or a plate and brush the cut side of each tomato with the olive oil mix. Oil that the Traeger Grill grate. Organize the lavender sprigs in a row, then vertical to the pubs of this Traeger Grill grate and marginally split, directly above the moderate flame.
- Put the tomatoes, cut side down, on top of the rosemary. Us tongs, gently turn the tomatoes cut side up, and brush off some of those charred rosemary leaves. Brush the tomatoes liberally using the olive oil mix. Cover and Traeger Grill till the berries are hot and tender but still hold their

shape, about two minutes more. Transfer to a heated serve platter or dinner plates and serve immediately, or keep warm until ready to serve.

Grilled Cherry Tomato Skewers
Ingredients

- 3 Tablespoons Extra-Virgin Olive Oil
- 8 7-Inch Bamboo Skewers, Soaked in Water For 15 Minutes, Then Drained
- 40 Cherry Tomatoes (About 1 Pint) 32 Large Fresh Basil Leave
- Kosher or Sea Salt
- Freshly Ground Pepper

Instructions

- Ditch the skewers before mild the Traeger Grill, so that they have loads of time. To build the skewers, thread 5 berries on each skewer, put a basil leaf, folded in half crosswise, involving the berries. Arrange the skewers at a le layer on a rimmed back sheet and brush the berries liberally on all sides with olive oil. To make a trendy zone, then bank the coals to one side of this Traeger Grill or turn off one of those burners.
- Oil that the Traeger Grill grate. Put the skewers straight over the medium-hot flame and Traeger Grill, turn once, till light Traeger Grill marks show up on either side, about 30 seconds each side. Transfer the skewers into the cooler section of this Traeger Grill, pay, and Traeger Grill till the berries are warm but the skin has not blistered, 1 to 2 minutes more. Transfer the skewers into a function dish and season with pepper and salt. Serve hot or at room temperature.

Grilled Choy with Sesame Oil
Ingredients

- 2 Teaspoons Asian Sesame Oil
- Kosher or Sea Salt
- 8 Heads Baby Bok Choy, Halved Lengthwise
- 2 Tablespoons Canola or Grapeseed Oil
- Store-Bought Thai Peanut Sauce for Drizzle

Instructions

- Organize the bok choy in a le layer on a large, rimmed rear sheet. In a small bowl, combine the canola and sesame oils and blend well. Brush both sides of their crispy white stalks (not the green leaves) of this bok choy with the petroleum mix.
- Oil that the Traeger Grill grate. Put a very long strip of transparency about 6 inches wide, across the duration of this Traeger Grill. Organize the bok choy, cut down, and so the white stalks are straight above the medium-hot fire along with also the delicate green leaves are all remainder on the transparency, shielded from the flame.
- Switch and Traeger Grill until light brown Traeger Grill marks seem and the bok choy is crisp-tender when pierced with a knife, about two minutes more. Organize the bok choy halves, cut side up, on a heated platter and garnish with the skillet. Drink immediately.

Salted Grilled Eggplant with Herbs
Ingredients

- ½ Cup Extra-Virgin Olive Oil
- Purple Globe Eggplants (About 12 Ounces Each), Cut Crosswise Into ½-Inchthick Slices
- 1 Tablespoon Herbs De Provence, Crushed
- 1 Teaspoon Kosher or Sea Salt

Instructions

- Arrange the eggplant slices in a le coating on a large, rimmed back sheet. In a small bowl, combine the olive oil, herbs de Provence, and salt and blend well. Generously brush the eggplant slices on both sides with the oil mix.
- Oil that the Traeger Grill grate. Put the eggplant slices straight over the medium-hot flame, pay, and Traeger Grill until dark brownish Traeger Grill marks seem, 2-3 minutes. Turn, recuperate, and Traeger Grill until dim Traeger Grill marks seem and the pieces are tender when pierced with a knife, about 3 minutes more. Transfer to a heated serve plate and serve immediately, or keep warm until ready to serve.

Asian Grilled Eggplant with Mayonnaise
Ingredients

- ¼ Teaspoon Freshly Ground White Pepper
- 4 Purple Asian Eggplants (About 8 Inches Long), Stem Ends Trimmed, Halved Lengthwise
- ¼ Cup Mayonnaise

- 1 Tablespoon White Miso 1½ Teaspoons Asian Sesame Oil
- 1 Teaspoon Soy Sauce
- 5 Tablespoons Canola or Grapeseed Oil
- 2 Tablespoons Asian Sesame Oil
- Kosher or Sea Salt

Instructions

- Create the miso mayonnaise: In a small bowl whisk together the mayonnaise, miso, sesame oil, soy sauce, and pepper until well mixed. Set aside. Arrange the eggplant halves in a le coating on a large, rimmed back sheet. Generously brush both sides of each eggplant half together with the oil mix. Oil that the Traeger Grill grate.
- Put the eggplants, flesh side down, right above the medium hot flame. Cover and Traeger Grill till dark brownish Traeger Grill marks appear, about 3 minutes. Twist, re-cover, and Traeger Grill on the skin side until the eggplants are tender when pierced with a knife, about 3 minutes more. Arrange the eggplant halves, flesh side up, on a heated platter. Drizzle the sauce over the top, or pass the sauce in the table.

Traeger Grilled Acorn Squash
Ingredients

- ¼ Cup Packed Dark Brown Sugar
- 1 Teaspoon Kosher or Sea Salt, Plus More for Sprinkles
- 1 Teaspoon Freshly Ground Pepper
- ¾ Cup (1½ Sticks) Unsalted Butter
- ¼ Cup Pure Maple Syrup
- ¼ Cup Good-Quality Bourbon Whiskey Such as Maker's Mark
- 2 Acorn Squashes

Instructions

- Grill or preheat a gas Traeger Grill on medium high. In a small saucepan, melt butter over moderate heat. Pour or ladle 1/4 cup of the egg into a heatproof bowl or quantify cup and put aside. Add the maple syrup, brown sugar, 1 tsp salt, and the pepper into the butter from the pan and simmer until the sugar is melted.
- Remove from the heat, add the bourbon, and stir till smooth. Set aside and keep warm. Cut each squash in half lengthwise. Scoop out and discard the seeds and str s. Cut each half into thick wedges, either quarters or thirds, are contingent on the size of the skillet. Order the skillet into a s le coating on a rimmed back sheet and brush the wedges liberally onto the flesh side using all the reserved melted butter.
- Sprinkle with salt. To make a trendy zone, then bank the coals to one side of this Traeger Grill or

turn off one of those burners. Oil that the Traeger Grill grate. Put the skillet on the trendy side of this Traeger Grill, pay, and Traeger Grill until only start to caramelize in the borders and simmer, 15 minutes. Brush the wedges together with the bourbon-butter mix, re-cover, and Traeger Grill another five minutes. Brush the pliers, re-cover, and Traeger Grill until tender when pierced with a knife, about 5 minutes more. Transfer the skillet into a function dish and serve immediately, or keep warm until ready to serve.

Traeger Grilled Ratatouille
Ingredients

- 1 Large Purple Globe Eggplant (About 1 Pound), Stem End Trimmed, Cut
- Lengthwise Into ¾-Inch-Thick Slices
- 10 Large Fresh Basil Leaves, Coarsely Chopped
- 1 Tablespoon Tomato Paste
- Freshly Ground Pepper
- 2 Zucchinis, Ends Trimmed, Halved Lengthwise
- 1 Large Red Bell Pepper, Quartered Lengthwise, Seeded, And Defibbed
- 2 10-Inch Bamboo Skewers, Soaked in Water For 15 Minutes, Then Drained
- Cup Roasted Garlic-Flavored Olive Oil
- 1½ Tablespoons Herbs De Provence, Crushed
- ½ Teaspoon Kosher or Sea Salt, Plus More for Season
- ½ Pint Cherry Tomatoes
- 1 Walla Walla Or Other Sweet Onion, Cut Crosswise Into ½-Inch-Thick Slices

Instructions

- Ditch the skewers before mild the Traeger Grill, so that they have loads of time. Prepare a medium-hot fire in a charcoal Traeger Grill or preheat a gas Traeger Grill on medium high. In a small bowl combine the olive oil, herbs de Provence, and 1/2 tsp salt and blend well. Thread the berries on the skewers and arrange on a plate. Brush the tomatoes lightly with the oil mix. Organize the stay vegetables at a le layer on a large, rimmed back sheet and brush liberally on both sides with the oil mix. Oil that the Traeger Grill grate.

- Put all of the vegetables except the tomatoes right above the medium-hot flame, and Traeger Grill, flip once, till dark brown Traeger Grill marks look on either side along with the veggies are crisp-tender when pierced with a knife, 2-3 minutes each side. Tim will change slightly for every vegetable; observe carefully and flip the veggies as needed.
- Traeger Grill the skewered tomatoes in precisely the exact same time, turn them until their skin blisters, about two minutes total. Transfer the Traeger Grill ed vegetables except the tomatoes to some cut plank, and cut to 1/2-inch balls. Put into a large bowl. Twist the berries off the skewers and add to the vegetables in the bowl, together with the basil.
- Mix the tomato paste with 2 tbsp water to cut it, and then fold the diluted paste evenly to the vegetable mix. Season to taste with pepper and salt. Serve hot or at room temperature.

Grilled Eggplant Stacks with Fresh Mozzarella
Ingredients

- 2 Large Balls (8 Ounces Total) Fresh Mozzarella Cheese, Each Cut Into 4 Slices
- 4 Ounces Arugula
- 6 Large Fresh Basil Leaves, Stacked, Rolled Like A Cigar, And Cut Crosswise Into
- 1 Large Purple Globe Eggplant (About 1 Pound), Cut Crosswise Into 8 Thick Slices
- 3 Tablespoons Tuscan Extra-Virgin Olive Oil, Plus More for Drizzle
- Kosher or Sea Salt
- Freshly Ground Pepper

Instructions

- Prepare a medium-hot fire in a charcoal Traeger Grill or preheat a gas Traeger Grill on medium high. Arrange the eggplant Pieces in a le layer on a large, rimmed back Sheet and brush the pieces on Either side together with the 3 tbsp olive oil. Sprinkle with salt. Oil the Traeger Grill grate. Arrange the eggplant straight above the medium-hot fire, pay, and Traeger Grill till dark brownish Traeger Grill marks seem, 2-3 minutes. Twist, re-cover, and Traeger Grill until shadowy Traeger Grill marks appear, about 2 minutes more.
- Put a slice of mozzarella on top of each eggplant slice, re-cover, and Traeger Grill until the eggplant is tender when pierced with a Knife along with the cheese is melted and hot, about 3 minutes more. To serve, put One-fourth of the arugula in the

middle of each warmed meal. Top with two Eggplant pieces, overlap them slightly.

- Scatter the beer threads over the top. Drizzle about 1 tablespoon olive oil on the top of every function, and Garnish with honey. Drink immediately.

Potatoes Tossed with Extra-Virgin Olive Oil
Ingredients

- Kosher or Sea Salt
- Freshly Ground Pepper
- 1 To 1¼ Pounds New Red Potatoes, Halved
- 2 Tablespoons Tuscan Extra-Virgin Olive Oil, Plus More for Drizzle

Instructions

- Poke the potato wedges once together with the tines of a fork. Put the potatoes into a bowl and toss them with the two tbsp olive oil. To make a trendy zone, then bank the coals to one side of this Traeger Grill or turn off one of those burners. Oil that the Traeger Grill grate. Arrange the potatoes, cut side down, right over the medium-hot flame, pay, and Traeger Grill until dark brown Traeger Grill marks appear, about 4 minutes.
- Turn cut side up, re-cover, and Traeger Grill for 4 minutes more. Transfer the potatoes into the cooler section of this Traeger Grill, pay, and Traeger Grill until tender when pierced with a knife, about 10 minutes more. Transfer the potatoes to a bowl that is serve. Drizzle with olive oil, sprinkle with fleur de promote, and throw.

CPSIA information can be obtained
at www.ICGtesting.com
Printed in the USA
BVHW052152130421
604817BV00010B/959